Even More Christmas Creations

10 SEASONAL PIANO FAVORITES
Arranged by RANDALL HARTSELL

T0079545

Dedicated to my editor, Charmaine Siagian

ISBN 978-1-70510-331-9

WILLIS MUSIC

EXCLUSIVELY DISTRIBUTED BY

HAL•LEONARD®

© 2020 by The Willis Music Co.
International Copyright Secured   All Rights Reserved

For all works contained herein:
Unauthorized copying, arranging, adapting, recording, Internet posting, public performance,
or other distribution of the music in this publication is an infringement of copyright.
Infringers are liable under the law.

Visit Hal Leonard Online at
www.halleonard.com

Contact us:
Hal Leonard
7777 West Bluemound Road
Milwaukee, WI 53213
Email: info@halleonard.com

In Europe, contact:
Hal Leonard Europe Limited
42 Wigmore Street
Marylebone, London, W1U 2RN
Email: info@halleonardeurope.com

In Australia, contact:
Hal Leonard Australia Pty. Ltd.
4 Lentara Court
Cheltenham, Victoria, 3192 Australia
Email: info@halleonard.com.au

PREFACE

The traditional melodies of Christmas offer musicians a rich fabric of material that spans hundreds of years of time and history.

Personally, I never grow tired of hearing and playing Christmas repertoire. This music reflects our shared heritage that has comforted people through periods of prosperity and famine, peace and conflict, joy and sorrow, fear and tranquility, as well as despair and hope. These lasting melodies remind us of our shared destinies and the magic music offers to every soul.

Enjoy sharing or teaching this music with exuberant expectation. Notes can shape our minds and hearts for the best that is yet to come.

Randall Hartsell

CONTENTS

Away in a Manger
(Medley)

Arranged by Randall Hartsell

Andante

p

With pedal

mf *mp*

Music by James R. Murray

mf

© 2020 by The Willis Music Co.
International Copyright Secured All Rights Reserved

Music by Jonathan E. Spilman

Music by William J. Kirkpatrick

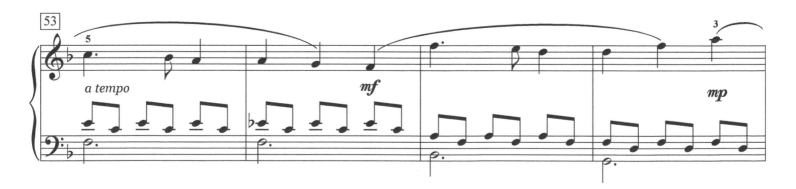

The First Noel

17th Century English Carol
Music from W. Sandys' *Christmas Carols*
Arranged by Randall Hartsell

© 2020 by The Willis Music Co.
International Copyright Secured All Rights Reserved

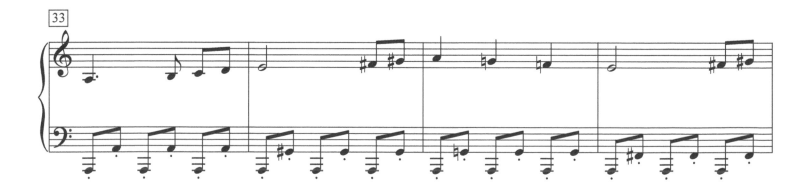

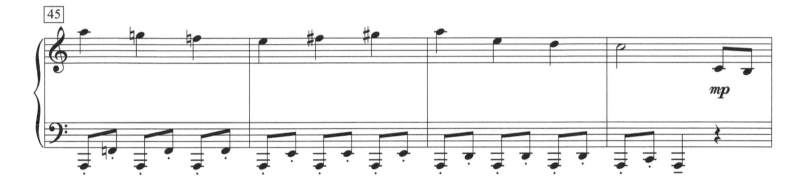

God Rest Ye Merry, Gentlemen

Traditional English Carol
Arranged by Randall Hartsell

© 2020 by The Willis Music Co.
International Copyright Secured All Rights Reserved

43 **Expressively**

meno mosso

47

mf

51

mp

55

60

p   *f*   *molto rit.*

In the Bleak Midwinter

Music by Gustav Holst
Arranged by Randall Hartsell

Slowly, from a distance

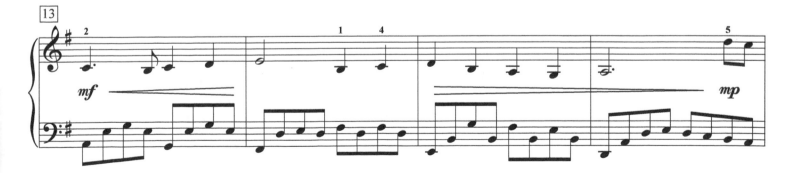

© 2020 by The Willis Music Co.
International Copyright Secured All Rights Reserved

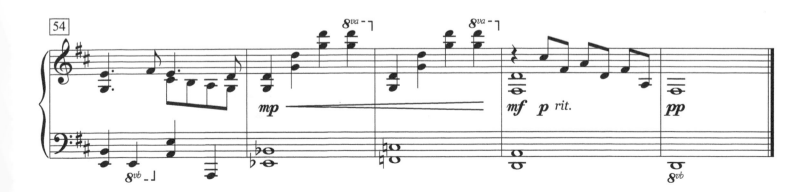

Here We Come A-Caroling

Traditional
Arranged by Randall Hartsell

© 2020 by The Willis Music Co.
International Copyright Secured   All Rights Reserved

O Christmas Tree

Traditional German Carol
Arranged by Randall Hartsell

Moderately, with energy

© 2020 by The Willis Music Co.
International Copyright Secured   All Rights Reserved

More slowly and freely

poco rit.   *mp*

With pedal

p

8ᵛᵇ

mf

mp

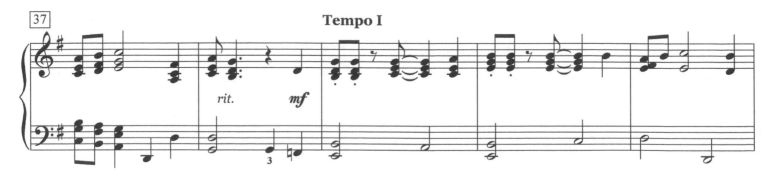

Tempo I

O Come, O Come, Emmanuel

15th Century French Melody
Arranged by Randall Hartsell

© 2020 by The Willis Music Co.
International Copyright Secured   All Rights Reserved

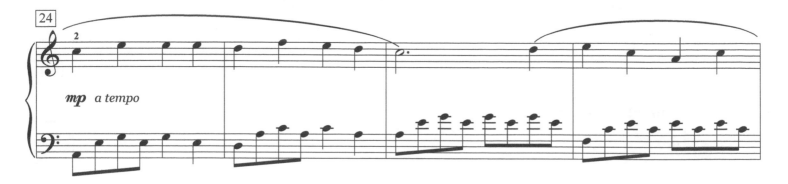

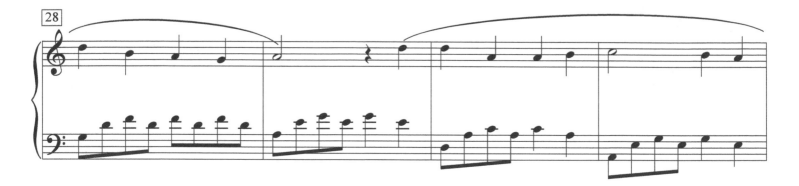

O Holy Night

Music by Adolphe Adam
Arranged by Randall Hartsell

© 2020 by The Willis Music Co.
International Copyright Secured All Rights Reserved

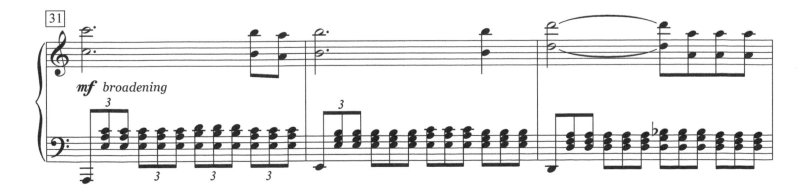

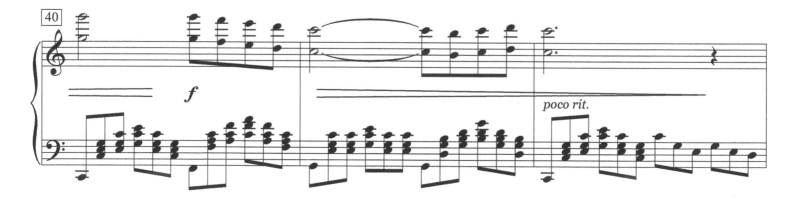

Silent Night

Music by Franz X. Gruber
Arranged by Randall Hartsell

© 2020 by The Willis Music Co.
International Copyright Secured   All Rights Reserved

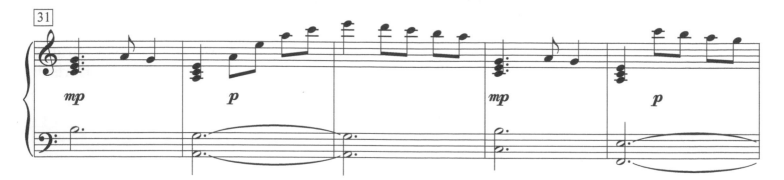

What Child Is This?

16th Century English Melody
Arranged by Randall Hartsell

Moderately

© 2020 by The Willis Music Co.
International Copyright Secured   All Rights Reserved

MORE PIANO SOLO ARRANGEMENTS
by Randall Hartsell

Hymn Creations

HL00416925
Amazing Grace • The Ash Grove
• Be Thou My Vision • Beach Spring (Lord, Whose Love In Humble Service) • Come, Thou Fount of Every Blessing • Fairest Lord Jesus • Holy, Holy, Holy • Kingsfold (My Soul Proclaims Your Greatness) • Now Thank We All Our God • When Morning Gilds the Skies.

More Hymn Creations

HL00122464
All Things Bright and Beautiful • Blessed Assurance • Break Thou the Bread of Life • Come, Thou Almighty King • Glorious Things of Thee Are Spoken • He Leadeth Me • Immortal, Invisible • Jesus, the Very Thought of Thee • My Hope Is Built on Nothing Less • 'Tis So Sweet to Trust in Jesus.

Even More Hymn Creations

HL00324185
Amazing Grace • For the Beauty of the Earth • Great Is Thy Faithfulness
Let Us Break Bread Together • Love Divine, All Loves Excelling • A Mighty Fortress Is Our God
There Is a Balm in Gilead • This Little Light of Mine • We Gather Together • Were You There?

Christmas Creations

HL00416823
Angels We Have Heard on High • Away in a Manger • Carol of the Bells • Deck the Hall • God Rest Ye Merry, Gentlemen • Good King Wenceslas • Jingle Bells • Joy to the World • O Come, Little Children • Silent Night • We Three Kings of Orient Are.

More Christmas Creations

HL00416916
Christmas Time Is Here • Do You Hear What I Hear • Here Comes Santa Claus (Right down Santa Claus Lane) • A Holly Jolly Christmas • I'll Be Home for Christmas • Let It Snow! Let It Snow! Let It Snow! • Rudolph the Red-Nosed Reindeer • Silver Bells • Wonderful Christmastime.

Wedding Creations

HL00113014
Air (Handel) • Allegro Maestoso (Handel) • Arioso (Bach) • The Heavens Declare (Marcello) • Jesu, Joy of Man's Desiring (Bach) • Love Divine, All Loves Excelling (Prichard) • Ode to Joy (Beethoven) • Rondeau (Mouret) • Trumpet Voluntary (Clarke). Plus 3 original pieces: Adagio from the Heart • Chanson d'amour • Unity of Love.

BIOGRAPHY

RANDALL HARTSELL is a composer, pianist/organist, clinician and teacher from Charlotte, North Carolina. Mr. Hartsell is particularly known for his lyrical and melodic compositional style, and consistently aims to write pieces that students will love to play and teachers will love to teach! He currently operates a private studio in the Charlotte area.

Mr. Hartsell is a graduate of East Carolina University, where he majored in piano pedagogy and performance, and was previously on the faculty of the school of music at the University of North Carolina (Charlotte). He has well over 100 publications in print, and has been featured as a commissioned composer in *Clavier* magazine.

Visit **www.halleonard.com** for more works by Randall Hartsell.